Christmas Gone Worng!

An All-Age Nativity Play

by

Fay Rowland

Copyright

Visit the author's website at www.fayrowland.co.uk

Typeset by Attic Studios, England
in Century Gothic

Published by Thomas Salt Books

ISBN: 9781915150080

Using This Script

Permission is hereby granted to the owner to make up to 30 copies of this script for rehearsal and performance in educational and faith settings. You must not sell the copies and they must be destroyed after use.

If you do not own this book, you may not copy it.

If you make a recording of your performance, you may place the video on a non-commercial personal, church, or school website or video channel. You must include the following copyright notice at the end of your video.

If you wish to use this script for any commercial purpose, please contact the author (fay@fayrowland.co.uk).

Images by Revd Ally Barrett. Please visit *reverendally.org* for more artwork, hymns and poems, and for permission to use.

Amazon reviews for 'God Is With Us – Everywhere!'

★★★★★ Phoebe

Totally recommend this easy to use, funny Nativity play

What an incredible gift this was for a Christmas during the coronavirus pandemic!

It is funny, easy to use and has quite a few small parts, which is great to get folks of all ages across the congregation involved. The parts were easily recorded separately and put together as a video.

We even managed to get the Moderator of the General Assembly of the Church of Scotland to play one of the wise men!

Fantastic resource and talented, helpful writer.

★★★★★ Katie

Excellent Nativity Script

Performed this online via video recordings - everyone loved it. A great, meaningful script, beautifully written. Funny in places and very moving.

★★★★★ Mrs K L Holt

Brilliant

This is brilliant. What an amazing alternative and fun way of telling the wonderful story of Jesus' birth and reminding us of how God is with us in all things.

Acknowledgements

My grateful thanks, as always, to my children for putting up with a mum who is always going 'tappity, tappity, tap' on the keyboard and forcing them to eat pizza for tea. (Not sure that they mind, really.)

Thanks also to my venerable alpha-reader, Steve D, and to all those who have given constructive criticism on this and other projects.

Enormous thanks to Ally for her wonderful artwork. You'll find snippets of her work on the cover and scattered around, ensuring that the sections start on the correct-facing pages and beautifying what would otherwise be blank spaces.

Thank you, finally, to those who support my writing ministry at The Reflectionary. The resources there are given away for free because I believe this stuff is important, but I do still need to make a living! If you have not visited yet, may I encourage you to pop along to www.reflectionary.org?

By buying this book you are helping me to continue so, for being part of the team, gentle reader, THANK YOU! You're a star!

(That's always assuming you've actually bought this book. If you haven't, why not?)

Christmas Gone Worng!

An All-Age Nativity Play

Christmas Gone Worng!

Welcome to this light-hearted Nativity play telling the traditional Christmas story with the help of carols, but where everything goes a bit *worng*. There is a stroppy Mary, a confused wise man and an angel who ... well, you'll have to read the script to find out.

The script incorporates readings from the gospels of Matthew, Luke and John in an easy-to-read translation.

The theme of the play is that God came to us at Christmas, despite things not being perfect. Immanuel, God With Us, even in our mess and muddle.

It is suitable for a school production such as a Nativity play or Christmas assembly, or at church as part of All-Age Worship, Messy Church, Crib Service or a Carol Concert.

Running time is approximately 22 minutes including readings, carol excerpts and talk, but excluding any songs or carols you may wish to add between scenes.

Cast

The script can be performed by a minimum of two payers, up to a cast of thirty or more. You can have adults, children or even puppets playing the roles.

Speaking Parts

- **MC**   Master of Ceremonies
- **Reader**   Reads Bible passage
- **Soloist**   Sings unaccompanied (could be recording)
- **Mary**   Stroppy teen
- **Joseph**   Irritated carpenter
- **Amos**   Shepherd's union rep
- **Bal**   Balthazar, wise man
- **Harold**   Angel, bit of a twit

Other players can be part of a choir (which does more than just sing) or non-speaking stable animals, stars, angels etc.

The script incorporates a seasonal message. This can be read by MC, or you could have a minister or head teacher step in at that point. You can replace the message with you own talk if you want.

Casting with Various Numbers

You can adapt the cast to suit your players, from 2 to 60.

If you have a limited number of people, one person can play several roles. There is time between the scenes for a single actor to change costume for the five named characters, although this will mean they cannot form a tableau on stage.

If you need to accommodate a large number of actors, the roles of shepherd and wise man can be split between three, either three speaking roles or one speaking and two non-speaking as preferred. You can also share the Bible readings between several readers. There are readings for each of the five scenes, so this can accommodate five, ten or fifteen readers.

Younger children can have non-speaking roles: as sheep accompanying the shepherds or as other stable animals, angels, stars etc, joining the tableau at the end for a truly Instagram-worthy scene.

In addition, the choir plays a vital role, more than simply leading congregational songs (if used). There really is a place for everyone!

Example casts

Cast of 2
- MC + all readings
- All other characters
- Soloist and choir are recordings, cast or live

Cast of 6

- MC + all readings
- Mary
- Joseph
- Amos
- Balthazar
- Harold
- Soloist and choir are recordings, cast or live

Cast of 10

- MC
- Reader
- Mary
- Joseph
- Amos
- Balthazar x 3
- Harold
- Soloist
- Choir is recordings, cast or live

Cast of 30+
(16/21/26 speaking + choir + non-speaking roles)

- MC
- Reader x 5 (or 10 or 15)
- Mary
- Joseph
- Amos x 3
- Balthazar x 3
- Harold
- Soloist
- Choir
- Non-speaking stable animals / angels / stars

Tableau

If you use different actors for the main characters, you can assemble a tableau on the stage, with each character joining it after their scene.

You will need a chair in the centre with enough space in front for the action, and a stool behind the chair.

Mary sits centre-stage after scene 1. Joseph stands beside her after scene 2. Amos and sheep kneel to one side after scene 3, and Balthazar to the other after scene 4. Harold stands on the stool at the end of scene 5.

Mary should surreptitiously produce baby Jesus, either from under / behind her chair or hidden in her clothes, ready for the final reveal in scene 5.

Small children sit with their appropriate characters to the sides and front so that they can be seen.

All tableau characters should lower their heads while other scenes are taking place so as not to distract the audience.

Non-speaking characters can enter at the same time as their speaking-part character, or at the start of Scene 5 together with children from the congregation dressed as characters. (Yes, even if that means three Marys and five wise men.)

You might like to have have spare shawls, head drapes (tea towels and rope ties) and tinsel crowns to give to children who don't have costumes.

Costume Suggestions and Props

MC   Master of Ceremonies
             Costume = modern dress

Soloist Preferably an angelic child, looking like a
             John Lewis advert
             Costume = traditional robes or Christmas
             jumper

Mary   Costume = hoodie and jeans, blue shawl
             over head, plus hidden baby for tableau

Reader   Costume = modern dress

Joseph   Costume = high-vis and hard hat with 'tea
             towel' headdress, plus hammer or saw

Amos   Shepherd
             Costume = overalls and 'tea towel'
             headdress, plus staff / toy sheep

Bal   Balthazar, wise man
             Costume = posh suit with bow tie, turban /
             fez, plus gift

Harold   Angel. Preferably an old man
             Costume = all white, with tinsel, halo and
             wings, plus tutu if at all possible

Hints and Tips

The words in square brackets and italics *[like this]* are stage directions. Don't read them out, do them!

Mary and Joseph should enter through the audience if possible, disturbing the soloist and choir. Amos and Balthazar can enter from opposite sides.

Balthazar needs to speak 'off stage' so will either need a microphone in the wings or should speak from a place where he can be heard.

For the tableau, place a chair centre stage for Mary, with a stool behind for Harold. You can hide a baby doll under or behind the chair.

If you have lighting available, dim the lights at the back as the tableau assembles, keeping the front lights high to draw attention to the actors for each scene. Raise the back lights as the tableau is revealed in scene 5.

To give younger children a larger part than simply joining the tableau at the start of scene 5, add a couple of rounds of 'Little Donkey' while they parade around the hall before taking their places on stage.

MC can have their words on a clip board or on a lectern, if needed.

Christmas Gone Worng!

The Script

Christmas Gone Worng

Scene 1 – Mary

MC *[In 'Christmas advert' voice]*

Christmas, the most perfect time of year.
A time of peace, joy and understanding
throughout the world.

A time when families never argue, when gravy is
never lumpy, and when Monopoly ends
harmoniously with everyone winning, even
Uncle Albert.

May I welcome you to our Nativity. We start in
the traditional manner, with a reading and a
carol telling the timeless story of our saviour's
birth.

Reading from Luke 1:26-38

God sent the angel Gabriel to Nazareth in
Galilee, to a young woman there. Her name
was Mary. She was engaged to Joseph who
was of David's family line.

The angel went into the house and said to her,
'Greetings Mary. God is pleased with you and is
with you!'

12

What the angel said troubled Mary. She wondered what this greeting meant.

The angel said to her, 'Do not be afraid, Mary. God has blessed you. You will have a baby son. Name him Jesus. He will be great and will be called the Son of the Highest One. The Lord God will make him king where his father David was king. He will be king for ever.'

Then Mary said to the angel, 'How can this happen? I have no husband.'

The angel answered, 'The Holy Spirit will come to you. The power of the Highest One will be over you. So the holy child born to you will be called the Son of God.

Mary said, 'I am the Lord's servant. Let it be as you have said.' Then the angel left her.

Soloist [formal and traditional]

🎼 Once in royal David's city,
Stood a lowly cattle shed,
Where a mother laid her baby,
In a manger for His bed:

[**Mary** enters from back, walking up aisle and making a fuss while singer continues]

🎼 Mary was that mother mild,
Jesus Christ, her little child.

Mary	Hold on! Hold on, just one tinsel-picking minute! What's all this about?
MC	What's all what about?
Mary	*[Indicating singer]* This! *[Indicating Christmas decorations]* This! *[Indicating congregation]* THIS!
MC	Ummn, we're celebrating Christmas. You know, when you had the special baby?
Mary	When I had the WHAT?
MC	God's son? Jesus? Ringing any bells?
Mary	*[Getting cross]* Huh? What are you on about? I ain't having no baby. Joseph and me have only just got engaged. We haven't even set the wedding day yet. Don't you go talking about some baby. You'll get people gossiping, and my Mum will never let me hear the end of it. *[Muttering to self – what a load of old cobblers, having a baby, talking rubbish, I'd get it in the neck for sure, etc]*
MC	Can I check, you are Mary, aren't you? From the carol. *You know, [Singing]* 🎵 'Mary was the mother mild ...'
Mary	*[Hands on hips]* Do I LOOK mild?

14

MC   *[Backing off]* Ummn, No?

Mary   And what's this about a cattle shed?

I'm sorry, but when I have a baby, I'm planning on midwives and a nice clean cot with fluffy blankets. And I ain't planning to give the baby a cow pat for a pillow!

MC   *[Cautiously]* Do you mind if I say something?

Mary   What?

MC   Well, it's just that you seem a bit more … stroppy that most Marys.

Mary   I'm a teenager, what do you expect? And if there's going to be pregnancy hormones on top of that, well, all I can say is there had better be a LOT of chocolate!

MC   Fair enough. I'll order a bulk pack.

Mary   You do that.

*[**Mary** exits if playing all characters, otherwise sits on stage to form start of tableau]*

Suggested songs

Silent Night
Mary, Did You Know?
Mary's Boy Child

Scene 2 – Joseph

Reading from Luke 2:1-7

> About that time, the Roman ruler Augustus made a law that everyone must have their names written in a register.
>
> Joseph left Nazareth, a town in Galilee, and went to Bethlehem in Judea. This was known as the town of David. Joseph went there because he was from the family of David. Joseph went to register with Mary because she was engaged to marry him and she was going to have a baby soon.
>
> While they were in Bethlehem, the time came for her baby to be born. This was her first child, a son. There were no guest rooms, so she wrapped him in cloths and laid him in an animal's food box.

Choir [keeping an eye out for trouble]

> Away in a manger
> No crib for a bed
> The little Lord Jesus
> Laid down his sweet head

[**Joseph** enters, making a fuss while choir sings]

> The stars in the bright sky
> Looked down where he lay

*[**Choir** fades off and stops when Joseph interrupts]*

🎼   The little Lord Jesus
             Asleep on the ...

Joseph   Oh no, no, no. We're not having any of that.
             Very bad for my social media presence, that is.
             Can't be doing with this kind of bad press. I'm
             on Check-a-Trader, I'll have you know!

MC   I'm sorry, you are ...?

Joseph   *[Pause, giving MC a 'what planet are you on?'*
             look]
             I'm Joseph. Who were you expecting, King
             flippin' Herod?

MC   No, no, of course you're Joseph. What's the
             problem, Joe? May I call you Joe?

Joseph   What's the problem? What's the problem, you
             ask? I'll tell you what the problem is.
             I've got a business to run. Got a wife and kid to
             support.
             And this kind of thing *[Indicating choir]* is bad for
             business. THAT'S what the problem is.

*[**Choir** looks offended]*

MC   You don't like the choir? But I thought they were
             rather good.

Joseph   Not the choir. It's what they're singing. Makes
             me look bad.

MC   What do you mean?

Joseph   Well, listen to the words. 'Away in a manger ...'

MC   *[Shrugs]*

Joseph   '... No crib for a bed.'

MC   *[Shrugs]*

Joseph   Well do you think I hadn't made one? Do you think I planned for my kid to spend his first night in some wonky old food box from the back of the stable?

It didn't even have proper dovetail joints. Splinters everywhere, and had they oiled it and carved a little teddy into the headboard like I had done? Oh no. Just a box. That's what my son got.

And one of the legs was longer that the others so it wobbled like Gran after a couple of sherries.

MC   *[Helpfully]* I suppose that helped rock the baby to sleep.

Joseph   *[Glares]*

MC   But no, no, I see how that must be very frustrating. You wanted to provide for your son, but you weren't able to.

Joseph   *[Deflated]* No, nor my wife. I mean, what kind of a husband carts his wife halfway across the country when she's about to pop, eh? And then when we got there, I couldn't even get a proper room for her to have the baby in.

That wasn't how I meant it to be. I'm such a failure. I bet God wishes he'd picked a different step-dad for his kid.

MC   Now, I'm sure that's not true, Joe. Didn't God send an angel to tell you to marry Mary?

Joseph *[Still looking glum]* Yes, I suppose he did.

MC   So there you go. You'll be fine as a dad, I'm sure. And anyway, you're not the only one who messes up in this story. You should see some of the gaffs that other people make!

Joseph *[Agreeing]* Yeah, tell me about it!

           [Pause]

           No, I mean actually tell me about it. Do the Bible bit.

MC   Oh right, yes.

*[**Joseph** exits if playing all characters, otherwise joins tableau]*

Suggested songs

Infant Holy, Infant Lowly
Calypso Carol (See Him Lying on a Bed of Straw)
Like a Candle Flame (God is With Us, Alleluia)

Scene 3 – Amos

[if using 3 shepherds, split parts as indicated]

Reading from Luke 2:8-16

> In the same part of the country, shepherds were in the field watching their sheep at night. An angel of the Lord came to them and a bright light from the Lord shone all around them. They were very much afraid.
>
> The angel said to them, 'Fear not! Listen, I bring you good news! This news will make you very glad. It is for all people. A saviour has been born for you today in David's town. He is Christ the Lord. This is the way you will know him. You will find a baby wrapped in a cloth, lying in a food box.'
>
> All at once a great number of angels from heaven were with the angel. They praised God and said, 'Praise God in the highest heaven! Peace on earth and loving mercy towards all people!'
>
> The angels left them and went back to heaven. The shepherds said to one another, 'Let us go to Bethlehem and see what has happened. It is the Lord who has told us about it.' They went quickly. They found Mary and Joseph, and the baby lying in the food box.

Choir   *[with Amos in choir being silly]*

🎼   While shepherds washed their socks by night,
            And hung them on the line,
            The angel of the Lord came down,
            And said, 'Those socks are mine!'

*[**Choir** dissolves into confusion, looking at their music]*

*[**Amos** enters from choir]*

Amos1   Heh, heh, heh! Finally got someone to sing the proper words.

MC   What *[Indicating choir]* was that?
            What did you do the choir?

Amos2   Oh, just changed a few words here and there. Much more fun, don't you think?

MC   I suppose, but the choir seems a little traumatised.

Amos3   They'll get over it. Anyway, I can't stand the normal words.

MC   What's wrong with the normal words? I think they're lovely.

Amos1   You wouldn't think they were so lovely if you'd been seated on the ground all night with rheumatism like mine.

            Cold, damp grass – it's no good for the joints, you know. Give me a nice, comfy armchair any day. And a big slice of pizza.

MC   *[Stage whisper to Amos]* I don't think you had pizza back then.

Amos2   *[Waving away the objection]* Details. Details.

Amos, by the way. Amos bar Laban.
[Offering hand] Union rep for the AA.

MC   Alcoholics Anonymous?

Amos3   Noooo, you twonk! It's our union, Amalgamated Agriculturals, incorporating:

Amos1   BURP, the Bethlehem Union of Reapers and Planters;

Amos2   SPIT, the Society of Ploughing Industry and Technology;

Amos3   and SNOT, the Shepherding, (brackets, Night-time) Operations Team.

Amos1   Anyway, the union will be balloting members about possible strike action next week.

MC   What? Why?

Amos2   We'd rather it didn't come to that, of course, but we have to look after the workers, especially in the light (no pun intended) of a recent incident.

MC   *[Looking confused]* What are you talking about? What about the workers?

Amos3   For the compensation, of course.

Displaced sheep, loss of working hours, trauma and mental anguish caused by sudden fright, and don't get me started on the health and safety!

MC   Oh, I see. Yes, it does sound like there are issues that need addressing. What can we do to help?

Amos1   I'm glad you asked.

Here's the list of requirements to bring our working conditions into line with government regulations:

[Consults list, either real or pretend, hands list to other Amoses if using a split role]

1 – that appropriate seating be provided for shepherds including orthopaedic chairs for those with back problems.

Amos3   2 – that in periods of inclement weather, shepherds be permitted to watch their flocks in centrally-heated observation huts via remote CCTV.

Amos3   3 – that the Angel of the Lord be reminded that, before the commencement of shining all around, he should ascertain that all those in the vicinity have been issued with, and donned, protective eyewear capable of filtering out the harmful effects of UV-A, UV-B and glory.

MC   That all seems perfectly reasonable to me. Is that everything?

Amos1   And we'd quite like an automatic sock-washer.

Amos2   But only if there's room in the budget.

MC   I'll see what I can do. Can I get back to the story now?

Amos3 Be my guest.

*[**Amos** exits if playing all characters, otherwise joins tableau]*

Suggested songs

Angels from the Realms of Glory
The First Nowell
O Holy Night

Scene 4 – Balthazar

[if using 3 wise men, split parts as indicated]

Reading from Matthew 2:1-11

> After Jesus was born, wise men from the east came to Jerusalem. They asked, "Where is the baby who was born to be king of the Jews? We saw his star as it rose and have come to worship him."

> The star went before them until it stopped above the place where the child was. When the wise men saw the star, they were filled with joy. They went to the house and saw the child with his mother, Mary.

> The wise men bowed down and worshipped the child. They opened the gifts they brought for him and give him treasures of gold, frankincense, and myrrh.

Bal1   *[Offstage]* Hang on a minute, I'm having trouble with my ... ooh ...

Bal2   *[Offstage]* That's a bit snug ... I just need to ... urggh, that's better.

Bal3   *[Offstage]* Anyone seen my shoes?

Bal1   *[Offstage]* Could you pass me the ... aaah ...

Bal2   *[Offstage]* Ooh! Careful where you put that ...

Bal3   *[Offstage]* Caught me right in the beg-your-pardon ...

[Continue in quieter voice while MC talks over – of course I've not put on weight, it shrunk in the wash, that's all ... well I don't know where you put it ... etc]

MC   Ahem, apologies for this, ladies and gentlemen. It seems that some of the cast have *[Addressing door where Balthazar will enter]* **FORGOTTEN TO TURN THEIR MIC OFF!**

Bal1,2,3   *[Offstage]* Oh, sorry. *[Click]*

MC   Ummn, right, well, err. It seems there might be a short delay, so we could, ummn, we could ... I know! How about a rousing chorus of Jingle Bells?

Choir   Batman smells!

MC   Noooo, no, no, no! Don't start that. Alright, not Jingle Bells. We could do, err ...

*[**Balthazar** enters in a hurry, adjusting headdress]*

Bal1   It's alright, it's alright.

Bal2   I'm here now, luvvies.

Bal3   Not too late, I hope?

MC   *[Loud whisper, trying to shoo him/them off]* You're too early. You're not due on until after the choir.

Reading first, then the choir, then it's you.

Bal1 Oh, right you are. I'll just pop back here.
[Goes into corner, but comes straight back out]
You won't even know I'm here.

MC Thanks.

Bal2 *[Popping back out]* I'll be quiet as a mouse.

MC Great.

Bal3 *[Popping back out]* Not that I'm saying there are mice around, you understand.

MC Yes, yes. Understood.

Bal1 *[Popping back out]* Ooh, just one tiny, weensy, little thing ...

MC *[Starting to get annoyed]* Yes?

Bal2 I've been listening to the choir ...

MC *[More annoyed]* Yes?

Bal3 and I heard what they sang last time ...

MC *[Penny drops]* Ah. Right.

Bal and I think,
[Posh voice] given my regal bearing and position of importance within the higher echelons of society,

Bal2 *[Posh voice]* plus the cultural significance of my elevated status,

Bal3 *[Common voice]* that they shouldn't go messing around and singing silly words about me.

MC Certainly, Mr Balthazar, sir. I'll make sure the choir behave themselves.
[Pointed look at choir, with 'I'm watching you' signs]

Choir *[Singing with exaggerated beauty]*

We three Kings of Orient are,
One in a taxi, one in a car,
One on a scooter, beeping his hooter,
Following yonder star.

Oh - star of wonder, star of light,
Sit on a box of dynamite,
Fly like a rocket, flames from your pocket,
You'll be a satellite.

*[**Choir** sniggers and looks guilty]*

Bal1 *[Marches to centre, arms folded and tapping foot]* What did I say? Hmm? What did I say?

MC *[Hanging head]* You said no silly words.

Bal2 No silly words. Exactly. And what did I get?

MC Silly words.
I'm sorry. I think Amos got at the choir again

*[**Amos** makes a rude face if onstage]*

Bal3 Amos, was it, eh? You just wait until this is over, Amos. I'll get my revenge. It'll be this *[Miming boxing]* and that for you. You just wait and see.

MC	Now, now Balthazar. It's Christmas. It's a time for peace, not for fighting.
Bal1	I'll give him peace, if I see that Amos. Peas and carrots all over his head. *[Boxing while being restrained by MC]*
Bal2	I'll make mincemeat of him. He's a right turkey. I'll give him a good stuffing.
Bal3	He's crackers if thinks he'll get away with this. I'll cream him to mash. I'll bash him in the mince pies. I'll … I'll
MC	*[Pulling Balthazar back]* Calm down, calm down. We don't want fisticuffs. This is a family show.
Bal1	But … but … *[Suddenly sagging]*
Bal2	Oh, I'm sorry. I'm so sorry. I don't really want to fight Amos. I'm rubbish at boxing anyway.
Bal3	It's just … *[Voice quavering]* … It's just …
MC	What is it, Balthazar?
Bal1	*[Bursting into tears]* It's the myrrh! *[Sobbing, like Myrr-rrr-rrr-rrh]*
MC	There, there. It's alright. Myrrh is a lovely gift.
Bal2	No it's not. It's a stupid gift. I should have brought nappies or baby clothes or a nice casserole. Even gold would have been useful, and frankincense is good for masking the smell. But

noooooo. I had to get all posh and bring myrrh. What the heck use is that for a baby?

MC   Yes, I see.

Bal3   And then the camel ran out of fuel on the way here, and that made me late. And then I couldn't find my shoes and I missed my cue, and then when the choir sang that ... [*Sobbing*]

MC   ... it was all just too much. Yes, I understand. Why don't you go and have a nice sit down, Balthazar? I'm sure the choir and Amos are [*Addressing choir*] **very sorry, aren't you**?

[**Choir** and **Amos** look sorry]

[**Balthazar** exits if playing all characters, otherwise joins tableau]

Suggested songs

From Heaven You Came (The Servant King)
In the Bleak Mid-winter
As with Gladness Men of Old

Scene 5 – Harold

Reading from John 1:1-14

> In the beginning was the Word.
> The Word was with God, and truly was God.
> From the very beginning, the Word was with
> God.
>
> Through this Word, God created all things.
> Nothing that was made, was made without him.
>
> Everything that was made received life from
> him, and his life gave light to everyone.
>
> This light is shining in the darkness,
> and darkness will never put it out.
>
> The Word became a human being,
> and made his home among us.
>
> We saw his true glory,
> the glory of the only Son of the Father,
> full of all God's kindness and truth.

[Adapt this section to invite children who are dressed as characters to join or form the tableau. Alternatively, have the speaking characters form the tableau, or show a picture on a screen.]

MC   And now, as we near the end of our Nativity, I'd
          like to invite anyone to join our tableau. You
          could be Mary or Joseph, a shepherd, wise man
          or angel, or even one of the stable animals.
          [Arrange children on stage]

What a lovely picture this is of the first Christmas. I'm sorry that we had so many interruptions to the story.

*[**Harold** sidles on, MC tries to ignore him]*

I had hoped our Nativity would go a bit more smoothly than this, but things don't always happen the way we plan, do they?

Still, despite all the mess, we made it to the end. So all that remains is for me to wish everyone here the very best of Christmas blessings as we come to our final …

*[**Harold** sidles right up to MC]*

MC   I'm sorry. Can I help you?

Harold I'm Harold. I'm an angel.

MC   I can see that. *[Face falls]* Oh, hang on. You don't mean Harold as in 'Hark the **Harold** Angels sing', do you?

Harold *[Brightly]* Yes!

MC   *[Emphatically]* No!
Just, no. We don't need Harold angels.
It's just getting silly now.

[Losing it]

This was supposed to be a proper Nativity story, but everything's gone wrong.
Next thing you know it'll be 'most highly-flavoured gravy' and wise men on scooters beeping their hooters.

Choir   We've already had that joke.

MC   *[Shoulders sag]*
You know what? I give up. I give up trying to make this work.
It's been one thing after another going wrong and I give up.

> *[If you want a minister or head teacher to give the talk, they take over here, amending first line of the talk below to:*
>
> Never mind. You sit down for a moment. I know you wanted a nice, traditional Nativity and nothing went to plan.
>
> *Feel free to substitute your own talk in this section]*

I just wanted a nice, traditional Nativity and nothing went to plan.

Mind you, that was the same for the people in our story too.

Look at Mary. She didn't plan to have her baby in a borrowed shed. It was smelly and draughty and miles away from her home and family. It's not exactly what a young mum dreams of, is it?

And Joseph. What a massive guilt-trip. The whole journey was down to him, and he couldn't even find his wife a decent house to have a baby in. The carpenter who couldn't provide a bed for his son. He must have been chewed up inside.

The shepherds got in a mess, too. Maybe they weren't thinking straight because of the angels, but leaving the sheep alone wasn't a great idea. I wonder how many went missing while they were away, and I wonder how much trouble they got into.

And poor old Balthazar. I understand why he lost his temper. He was stressed up to the eyeballs and it all got too much for him.

They're not very different from us, really. How many of us plan a perfect Christmas only to find that, like Mary, things don't work out how we'd hoped? Or, like Joseph, we feel a failure because we can't do what we think is expected of us. Like the shepherds, we make bad decisions and then have to deal with the fall out. Like Balthazar, we have high expectations of the festivities and of ourselves, and the pressure all gets a bit much.

Real life isn't like the Christmas adverts. Real life is, if we're honest, a bit of a mess.

So this Christmas, I have some Good News. Good News for you. Good News for me. Good News, as the angels said, for the whole world.

God's OK with mess.

The reading we've just heard, from the start of John's Good News, says that God made his home with us. Right here in the mess and the stuff that didn't work out as planned.

God With Us. That's what the word Immanuel means – it's one of the names we give to Jesus. Jesus is God With Us. Right here. Right now.

God knows about the plans that didn't work out. God knows about the gnawing guilt. God knows about the bad decisions. God knows about the sadness behind the smile. And you know what? God still loves you.

And that's very Good News

[Turning to Harold / MC re-enters]

MC   So, Harold? You come right on in. I'm sorry I snapped at you. It's not been the Nativity I hoped for, but that's not your fault.

*[**Harold** joins tableau]*

Let's go with Hark the Harold Angels and rejoice that God really is with us, even with our messy lives and lumpy gravy.

And a Merry, Messy Christmas to us all.

All   *[waving]*
Merry Christmas!

Suggested songs

Hark the Herald Angels Sing
It Came Upon the Midnight Clear
Light of the world (Here I am to Worship)
Shine, Jesus, Shine
O Come All Ye Faithful

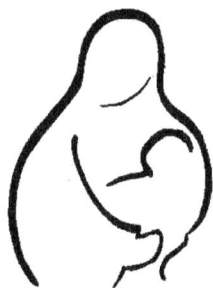

About the Author

Hi, I'm Fay.

In no particular order, I am a mum, choc-o-holic, mathematician, author, blogger, knitter, children's worker and mad scientist.

I write The Reflectionary, a weekly blog of original resources for churches, youth groups, children's work and schools' ministry.

Everything is free, so pop along and help yourself at www.reflectionary.org. You can sign up there to have the posts sent straight to your mailbox. No spam ever, I promise!

I studied Theology at Spurgeon's College and at Wesley House, Cambridge, specialising in children's spirituality, and I'm a trainee Lay Minister in the Church of England. You can find links to my published books and academic works at www.fayrowland.co.uk.

When not writing or studying, I teach maths for a living and spend most of the rest of the time being creative. I worship with a large Anglican church in the Midlands.

I live with my children and pet dragon in an untidy house full of noise and glue sticks and mess (which I blame on the kids, but really, it's me).

Other Publications

A Bucketful of Ideas for Church Drama (the green one)

"Parables as Jesus would have told them – witty and thought-provoking."

"Thirty Pieces of Chocolate is a fine pun-run."

Amazon's chart-topper in Puppet Scripts.

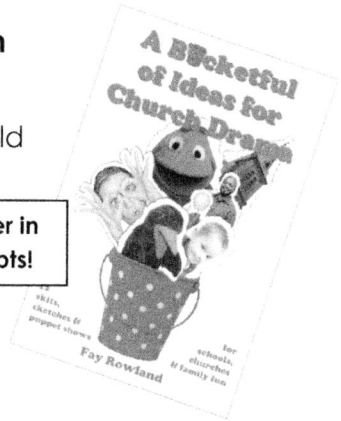

A(nother) Bucketful of Ideas for Church Drama (the blue one)

14 scripts including CRISP-tingle, a pop-up nativity, and lots more.

"Delivers the timeless truths of scripture in a modern and punchy manner."

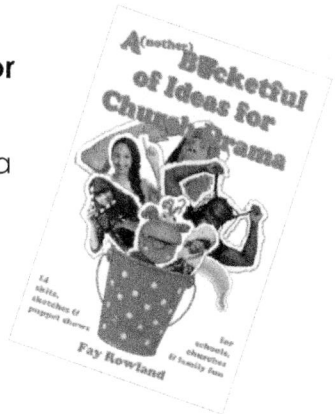

God Is With Us – Everywhere!

Featuring a cool Gabriel, terrified shepherds and three confused scientists, this witty yet poignant Nativity is perfect for your school or church production.

"Thank you for your script, we had it at our online carol service yesterday - and it went down a storm!"

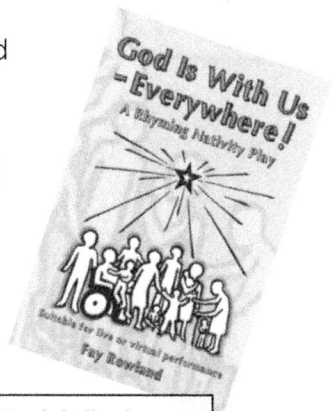

Walking to Bethlehem

25 imaginative devotions for adults and children, with reflective colouring and craft ideas.

"Travel from BC to AD to focus your mind on the road to Bethlehem. Fun and devotional, practical and creative."

#1 Best-Seller in Advent Devotions!

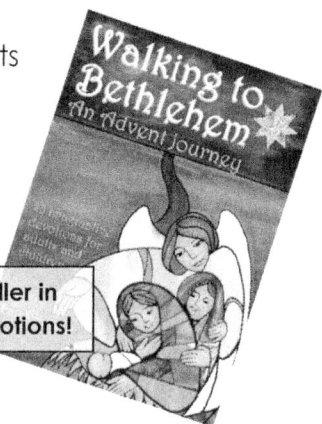

The Big Story

Discover the Bible as one big story of God and God's people, from the very beginning of everything up to the wonder of Easter.

Perfect for personal devotions, for weekly Bible studies and youth groups, discover The Big Story today.

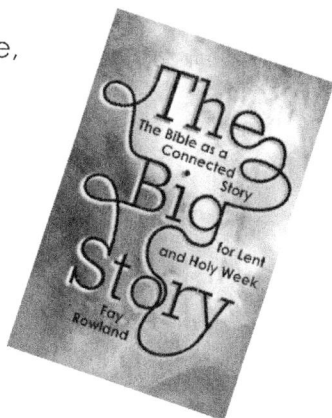

Broken Bits & Weirdness

Meet nine of the Bible's dismal failures and learn how God still loves them (and us), even with our Broken Bits & Weirdness.

With Bible notes, crafts, cooking, colouring and other resources, and studies for Good Friday and Easter Day, this is perfect for Lent or any time of year.

#1 Best-Seller in Bible Meditations!

Creativity Matters

Join thirteen authors as they share their passion for why you should write in their genre and find your own passion as you read.

In my chapter, 'Why Write Drama?', you can discover what makes drama sparkle, and why you shouldn't take your gran to see a Greek satyr play!

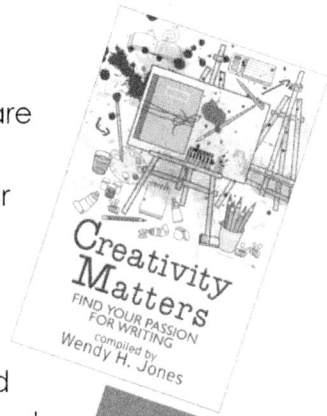

URC Prayer Handbooks

I have been a commissioned author for the URC's prayer handbooks for several years.

They are full of original, passionate, quirky and relevant prayers, with each Sunday having several prayers linked to readings from the Revised Common Lectionary. They are suitable for both congregational and private use, using contemporary language and covering a broad range of topics.

Available from the URC's website shop.

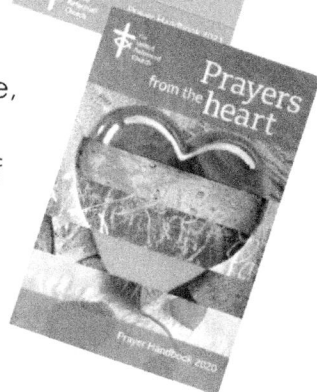

Printed in Dunstable, United Kingdom

66033872R00037